THE NOVELLO BOOK OF MUSIC *for*
LENT & EASTER

ANTHEMS AND HYMNS FOR LENT, HOLY WEEK & EASTERTIDE FOR MIXED-VOICE CHOIRS

Selected & edited by David Hill

Published by
Novello Publishing Limited
14-15 Berners Street,
London W1T 3LJ, UK.

Exclusive Distributors:
Music Sales Limited
Distribution Centre, Newmarket Road,
Bury St Edmunds, Suffolk IP33 3YB, UK.

Music Sales Corporation
180 Madison Avenue, 24th Floor,
New York NY 10016, USA.

Music Sales Pty Limited
Units 3-4, 17 Willfox Street, Condell Park
NSW 2200, Australia.

Order No. NOV310849
ISBN 978-1-78038-840-3

Music processed by Chris Hinkins and Paul Ewers Music Design.
Project Manager and Editor: Jonathan Wikeley.

Printed in the EU.

www.musicsalesclassical.com

THE NOVELLO BOOK OF MUSIC *for*
LENT & EASTER

ANTHEMS AND HYMNS FOR LENT, HOLY WEEK
& EASTERTIDE FOR MIXED-VOICE CHOIRS

Selected & edited by David Hill

NOVELLO

Introduction

The period of time from Lent, through Holy Week, to Easter Sunday is the most moving and holy journey of the Christian year. The sixty-four pieces in *The Novello Book of Music for Lent and Easter* have been chosen to offer a vibrant selection of pieces for all the major feast days from Ash Wednesday to Easter Sunday, as well as a generous selection of works for the seasons of Lent, Passiontide and Eastertide.

Great care has been taken to include interesting or new versions of standard texts—such as Svein Møller's beautiful setting of the *Ave verum*, Ralph Allwood's haunting *On the Mount of Olives* and Antonio Lotti's visceral six-voice *Crucifixus*— and arrangements of well-loved melodies, such as Stephen Jackson's *Lord of the Dance* and *Were you there?* and Dale Adelmann's *Steal away*. We have also carefully considered the amount of rehearsal required to learn a lot of music in a busy season. With this in mind, we have included a number of shorter and easily learnable anthems, such as J. C. Bach's *Es ist nun aus mit meinen Leben*, Benjamin Britten's *Corpus Christi Carol*, John Dowland's *An heart that's broken and contrite* and Charles Wood's *O for a lay!*, to name but four, which we hope will encourage choirs to introduce a wider range of anthems into their repertoire.

The role of music in worship is to enhance the liturgy, and we have endeavoured to think slightly outside the box on some occasions—to provide pieces that will make congregations sit up and listen—to which end we have occasionally considered slightly less traditional texts, or particularly striking settings. Adam Harvey's *Gethsemane*, Jonathan Wikeley's *A Thin Place* and Christopher Borrett's *The Two Adams* all offer engagingly different texts; Patrick Hadley's *My beloved spake* and Knut Nystedt's *Immortal Bach* (arranged here for three choirs) are hugely effective anthems for their occasions; while Charles-Marie Widor's *Surrexit a mortuis*, published here for the first time in a version for single organ and choir, provides an unforgettable opening to an Easter service.

We have commissioned several new hymn arrangements, from the reflective: James Burton's *It is a thing most wonderful* and Tom Wiggall's *When I survey the wondrous cross*; to the thrillingly dramatic: Matthew O'Donovan's *Jesus Christ is risen today*, Christopher Johns's *Ye choirs of new Jerusalem* and Richard Marlow's *Alleluia! Alleluia!*. All of these have been carefully composed to be musically interesting, yet easy for congregations to sing. In addition, a number of plainsong hymns and chants have been arranged for various occasions.

I am enormously grateful to my colleagues at Novello for their input, advice and expertise; in particular to Jonathan Wikeley, Daniel Rollison, Matthew Berry, Kate Johnson, Howard Friend, Chris Hinkins and Paul Ewers. Many other people contributed to the production of this book and I would particularly like to thank Stephen Disley, Maggie Hamilton, Paul Kennington, Peter Miller, Benjamin Nicholas, Kristina Radermacher, Samuel Rathbone, Geoffrey Webber and Carl Wikeley.

David Hill
Rutland, July 2013

Contents

Ash Wednesday

Lent & Passiontide

Palm Sunday

Maundy Thursday

Good Friday

Easter Vigil

Easter Sunday & Eastertide

In ieiunio et fletu

Joel 2: 12, 17

Thomas Tallis (1505-85)
ed. Lionel Pike

4

Miserere mei

from Psalm 51

Henry Purcell (1659-95)
ed. Anthony Lewis and Nigel Fortune

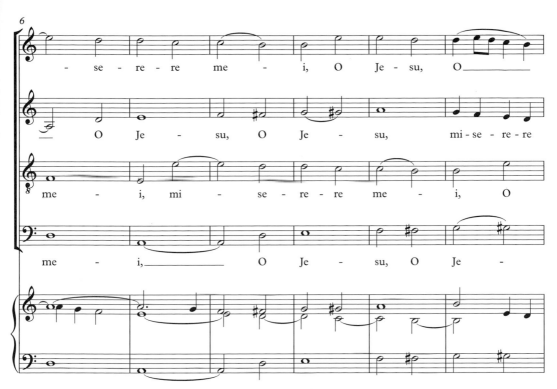

A Penitential Responsory

Psalm 51

Andrew Gant (b. 1963)

12

CANTOR

Make me a clean heart, O God: and renew a right spirit with - in me.

Cast me not away from thy presence: and take not thy Ho - ly Spi - rit from me.

S.
A.

f

Re-mem-ber, O man, that thou art dust, and un-to dust thou shalt re - turn.

T.
B.

f

CANTOR

O give me the comfort of thy help again: and stablish me with thy free Spirit.

Then shall I teach thy ways unto the wicked: and sinners shall be conver - ted un - to thee.

S.
A.

f

Re-mem-ber, O man, that thou art dust, and un-to dust thou shalt re - turn.

T.
B.

f

CANTOR

Deliver me from bloodguiltiness, O God, thou that art the God of my health:

and my tongue shall sing of thy righteousness.

SOPRANO
p

Re-mem-ber, O man, that thou art dust, and un-to dust thou shalt re - turn.

ALTO *p*

Re-mem-ber, O man, that thou art dust, and un-to dust thou shalt re - turn.

All in the April evening

Katherine Tynan (1859-1931)

Hugh S. Roberton (1874-1952)

18

Two stark cross-es be-tween, All in the A-pril ev - 'ning,— A-pril airs were a-

Two stark cross-es be-tween, All in the A-pril ev - 'ning, A-pril airs were a-

Two stark cross-es be-tween, All in the A-pril ev - 'ning, A-pril airs were a-

Two stark cross-es be-tween, In the A-pril ev-'ning, A-pril airs were a-

-broad; I saw the sheep with their lambs,— And thought on the Lamb of God.

-broad; I saw the sheep with their lambs, And thought on the Lamb of God.

-broad; I saw the sheep with their lambs,— And thought on the Lamb of God.

-broad; I saw the sheep with their lambs, And thought on the Lamb of God.

for John Hahessy

Corpus Christi Carol
from *A Boy was Born*

Anon. (15th century)

Benjamin Britten (1913-76)

This carol has been arranged by the composer from his Choral Variations for mixed voices *A Boy was Born* (CH76549). The words are from *Ancient English Christmas Carols* collected and arranged by Edith Rickert, and are reprinted by her kind permission and that of the publishers, Messers. Chatto and Windus.

The fal-con hath borne__ my make*__ a - way.   In that

or-chard there was__ an hall_____ That was hang-ëd with pur-ple and pall.__

a little cresc.

__ And in that hall there was__ a bed,_____ It was hang-ëd with

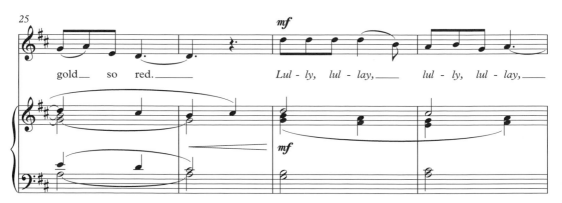

gold__ so red._____ Lul - ly, lul - lay,__ lul - ly, lul - lay,__

* mate

* maid

The fal - con hath borne my make a - way.

very quietly
And by that bed - side there stand - eth a stone,
Man.

Cor - pus Chri - sti writ - ten there - on.

ah ah

(without 4')

19 January 1961

Drop, drop, slow tears

Phineas Fletcher (1582-1650)

Kenneth Leighton (1929-88)

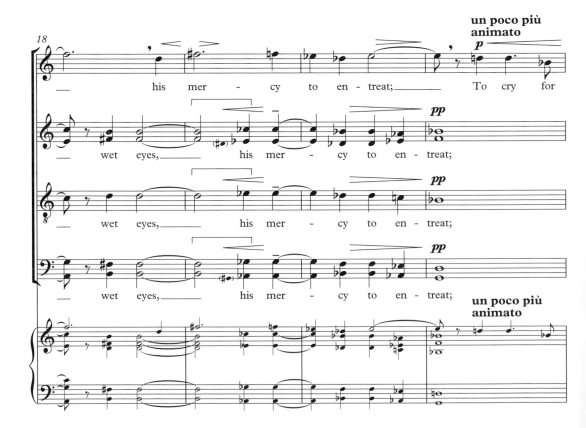

ven - geance _____ sin _____ doth nev-er cease. _____

To cry for ven - geance sin doth nev - er cease. _____

To cry for ven - geance sin doth nev - er cease. _____

To cry for ven - geance sin doth nev - er cease. _____

sostenuto e calmissimo

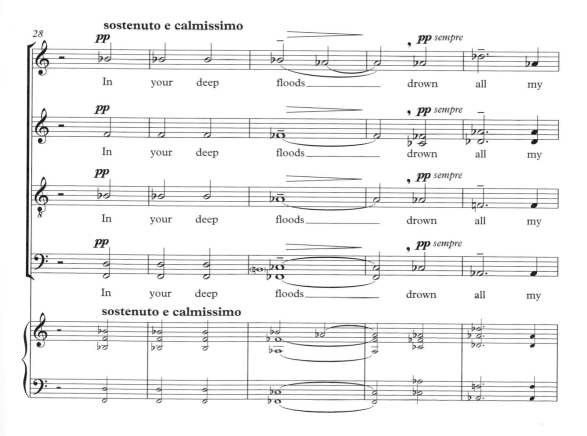

In your deep floods _____ drown all my

In your deep floods _____ drown all my

In your deep floods _____ drown all my

In your deep floods _____ drown all my

sostenuto e calmissimo

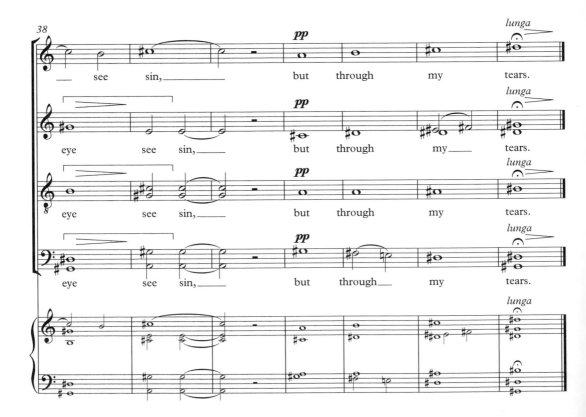

for RCMJD Chamber Choir

Drop, drop, slow tears

Phineas Fletcher (1582-1650)

Graham Ross (b. 1985)

Farnham, 16 May 2003

Es ist nun aus mit meinem Leben

Magnus Daniel Omeis (1646-1708)

Johann Christoph Bach (1642-1703)

es ist nun aus, es ist___ voll-bracht,
Nun ist es aus, es ist___ voll-bracht,
Mein Leid ist aus, es ist___ voll-bracht,
Was Je-sus macht, is wohl - ge-macht!

Welt, gu - te Nacht!

Welt, gu - te Nacht! Welt, gu - te Nacht!___ Welt, gu - te Nacht!

1. Now my life is ended,
God who gave it, takes it to him.
Not the smallest drop remains in the vessel,
no faint spark will now avail it, life's light
is extinguished. Not the least grain of sand
still runs through the glass,
it is now ended, it is accomplished,
world, good night!

2. Come, day of death, o sun of life,
you bring me more joy and bliss
than the day of my birth can bring,
you put an end to my suffering,
which before the joys of christening
was already begun.
Now it is ended, it is accomplished,
world, good night!

3. World, good night! Keep what is yours,
and leave Jesus as mine own,
for I will not leave my Jesus!
May God protect you, my dear ones,
let my death not grieve you,
since it has brought me such happiness;
my suffering is ended, it is accomplished,
world, good night!

4. Why would you grieve for me?
Ah, ease your tears,
for mine are eased already;
Jesus wipes them from my eyes;
what use then should yours be,
laugh with me like a child.
That which Jesus does is well done!
World, good night!

Forty days and forty nights

George Hunt Smyttan (1822-70)

Martin Herbst (1654-81)
Leighton George Hayne (1836-83)

1. For - ty＿ days and for - ty nights＿ Thou＿ wast fast-ing in＿ the wild,
2. Shall not＿ we thy sor - row share,＿ And＿ from earth-ly joys＿ ab - stain,
3. And if Sa - tan, vex - ing sore,＿ Flesh or spi - rit should＿ as - sail,

For - ty＿ days and for - ty nights; Tempt - ed＿ and yet un - de - filed.
Fast - ing＿ with un - ceas - ing prayer, Glad＿ with＿ Thee to suf - fer pain?
Thou, his＿ van - qui - sher be - fore, Grant＿ we＿ may not faint＿ or fail.

4. So shall we have peace di - vine, Ho - lier glad - ness ours shall be,
5. Keep, O keep us, Sa - viour dear, Ev - er con - stant by thy side,

Round us too shall an - gels shine, Such as mi - ni - stered to thee.
That with thee we may ap - pear At th'e - ter - nal Ea - ster - tide.

An heart that's broken and contrite

William Leighton (c.1565-1622)

John Dowland (1563-1626)
ed. Lionel Pike

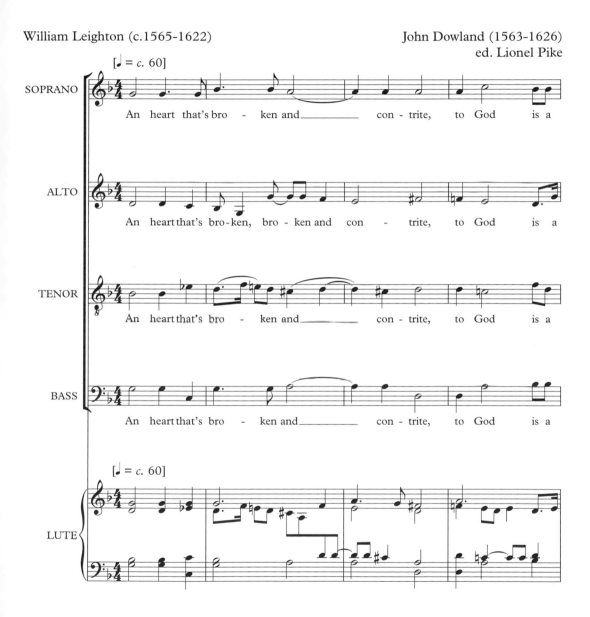

sweet, sweet sa - cri - fice: re - pent-ant sin - - ners
sweet, a sweet__ sa - cri - fice: re - pent - ant sin - ners__
sweet, a sweet_____ sa - cri - fice: re - pent - - ant sin - ners__
sweet sa - cri - fice: re - pent - - ant sin - ners

him de - light, far__ more, far__ more than just men in their sight.
him de - light, far_____ more, far more, more_ than just men in their_ sight.
him_ de - light, far__ more than just men, more_ than just men in their sight.
him de - light, far more, more than just men in their sight.

* Pause second time only

It is a thing most wonderful

W. Walsham How (1823-97)

Essex folksong
Vv 1 & 2 arr. Ralph Vaughan Williams (1872-1958)
Vv 3-5 arr. James Burton (b. 1974)

ORGAN

VOICES & ORGAN

1. It is a thing most won - der - ful, Al - most too
2. And yet I know that it is true: He chose a

won - der - ful to be, That God's own Son should
poor and hum - ble lot, And wept, and toiled, and

come from heaven, And die to save a child like me.
mourned, and died For love of those who loved him not.

3. But ev - en could I see him die, I could but

bear a lit - tle part Of that great love, which,

like a fire, Is al - ways burn - ing in his heart.

31 May 2013
Castlecroft

Jesu, dulcis memoria

Office hymn for the Feast of the Holy Name
St Bernard of Clairvaux (12th century)

attrib. Tomás Luis de Victoria
(1548-1611)

Immortal Bach

Anon.

Johann Sebastian Bach (1685-1750)
arr. Knut Nystedt (b. 1915)

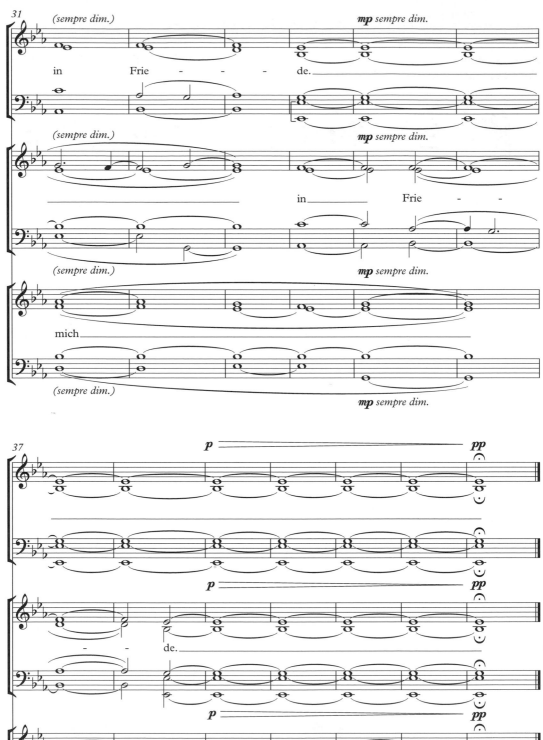

The Crown of Roses (Legend)

Russian poem
Trans. Geoffrey Dearmer (1893-1996)

Pyotr Ilyich Tchaikovsky (1840-93)

1. When Je-sus Christ was yet a child He had a gar - den small and

wild, Where-in he che-rished ro - ses fair, And wove them in - to gar-lands

there. 2. Now once,_ as_ sum - mer - time_ drew_ nigh,_ There came_ a_ troop_ of

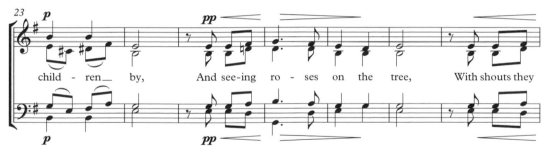

child - ren_ by, And see-ing ro - ses on the tree, With shouts they

My song is love unknown

Samuel Crossman (1624-83)

John Ireland (1879-1962)
Vv 3, 5 & 7 arr. Christopher Robinson
(b. 1936)

v.3 over page

1. My song is love un - known, My Sa-viour's love to me, Love
2. He came from his blest throne, Sal - va - tion to bes - tow: But

to the love - less shown, That they might love - ly be._____ O,
men made strange, and none The longed -for Christ__ would know._____ But

who am I, That for my sake My Lord should take Frail flesh, and die?
O, my Friend, My Friend in-deed, Who at my need His life did spend!

4. Why, what hath my Lord done?
   What makes this rage and spite?
   He made the lame to run,
   He gave the blind their sight.
   Sweet injuries!
   Yet they at these
   Themselves displease,
   And 'gainst him rise.

   v.5 over page

6. In life no house, no home,
   My Lord on earth might have;
   In death no friendly tomb,
   But what a stranger gave.
   What may I say?
   Heav'n was his home;
   But mine the tomb
   Wherein he lay.

   v. 7 over page

O languens Jesu

Szegedi (1674)

Lajos Bárdos (1899-1986)
Original tune: Szelepcsényi (1675)

1. O lan-guens Je - su, de-func-te Je - su, Ma-tris in si-nu flen - tis! Nos-tros do - lo - res, cor - dis a - mo - res Fac so-ci - os do-len - tis.
2. O Je-su cha - re, fac nos a - ma - re Te pro no-bis do-len - tem. Te nunc de-flen - do, te-cum do-len - do, Vi-de-bi - mus gau-den - tem.

Fac so - ci - os O Je - su!... Nos-tros do - lo - res, cor - dis a - mo - res Fac so-ci - os do-len - tis.

Vi - de-bi - mus O Je - su!... Te nunc de-flen - do, te-cum do-len - do, Vi-de-bi - mus gau-den - tem.

A - men.

1930

O Saviour of the world

from The Visitation of the Sick,
Book of Common Prayer

Frederick Arthur Gore Ouseley
(1825–89)

Oculus non vidit

1 Corinthians 2: 9

Daniel Rollison
(b. 1988)

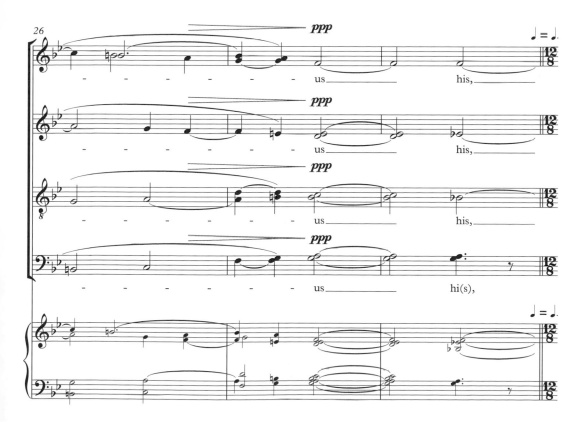

2009 rev. 2013

Pange lingua (1)
(Of the glorious body telling)

St Thomas Aquinas (1227-74)
Trans. J. M. Neale (1818-66)
and others

Mode iii
arr. David Hill (b. 1957)

vv. 1 & 6 FULL
vv. 3 & 5 TENORS & BASSES

Omit melody when accompanying T.B. verses

1. Of the glo-rious bo-dy tell - ing, O__ my tongue, its mys-t'ries sing,__
3. At the last great sup-per ly - ing Cir - cled by his cho-sen band,__
5. There-fore we, be-fore him bend - ing, This__ great sa-cra-ment re - vere:__
6. Glo - ry let us give and bles - sing To__ the Fa - ther and the Son,__

And the blood, all price ex-cell-ing, Which the world's e-ter-nal King,__
Du - ly with the law com-ply-ing, First he fi-nished its com-mand,__
Types and sha-dows have their end-ing, For the new-er rite is here;__
Ho-nour, might and praise ad-dres-sing, While e-ter-nal a-ges run;__

vv. 2 & 4 over page

In a spot-less womb once dwell-ing, Shed for this world's ran-som-ing.
Then, im-mor-tal food sup-ply-ing, Gave him-self by__ his own hand.
Faith, our out-ward sense be-friend-ing, Makes the in-ward__ vi-sion clear.
Ev - er too his love con-fes-sing, Who, from both, with__ both is one.

A - men.__

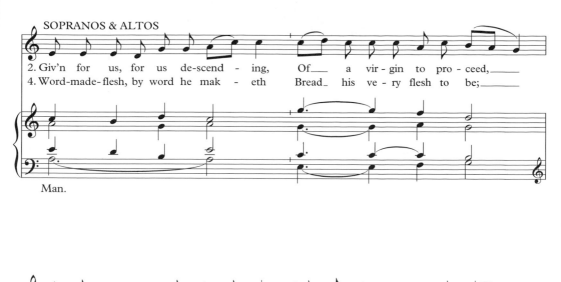

SOPRANOS & ALTOS

2. Giv'n for us, for us de-scend - ing, Of__ a vir-gin to pro-ceed,__
4. Word-made-flesh, by word he mak - eth Bread_ his ve - ry flesh to be;__

Man.

Man with man in con-verse blend-ing, Scat-tered he the gos - pel seed,__
Man in wine Christ's blood par - tak - eth: And if sen - ses fail to see,__

vv. 3, 5 & 6 on previous page

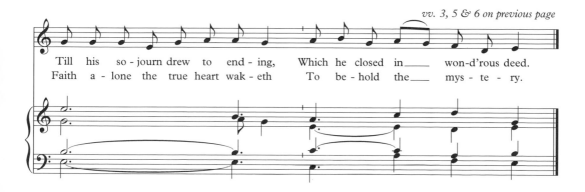

Till his so - journ drew to end - ing, Which he closed in____ won-d'rous deed.
Faith a - lone the true heart wak - eth To be - hold the____ mys - te - ry.

Pange lingua (2)

(Sing, my tongue, the glorious battle)

Venantius Fortunatus (530-609)
Trans. Percy Dearmer (1867-1936)
and J. M. Neale (1818-66)

Mode iii
arr. David Hill (b. 1957)

vv. 1, 4 & 8 FULL
v. 2 TENORS & BASSES

1. Sing, my tongue, the glo-rious bat - tle, Sing__ the end-ing of the fray,__
2. God in pi - ty saw man fall - en, Shamed_ and sunk in mi - se - ry,__
4. Thir-ty years a-mong us dwell - ing, Now__ at length his hour ful - filled,__
8. To the Tri - ni - ty be glo - ry, To__ the Fa - ther and the Son,__

Omit melody when accompanying T.B. verses

O'er the Cross, the vic-tor's tro - phy, Sound the loud tri - um-phant lay:__
When he fell on death by tast - ing Fruit of the for - bid - den tree:__
Born for this, he meets his Pas - sion, For that this he free - ly willed,__
With the co - e - ter - nal Spi - rit Ev - er three and ev - er One,__

v. 3 over page

Tell how Christ, the world's Re - deem - er, As a Vic - tim__ won the day.
Then a - no - ther tree was cho - sen Which the world from__ death should free.
On the cross the Lamb is lift - ed, Where his life - blood__ shall be spilled.
One in love and one in splen-dour, While un - end - ing__ a - ges run.

Tenors and Basses
5. Bend thy boughs, O Tree of Glory,
   Thy too-rigid sinews bend;
   For awhile the ancient rigour
      That thy birth bestowed, suspend,
   And the King of heavenly beauty
      On thy bosom gently tend.
v.6 over page

Full
7. He endured the nails, the spitting,
      Vinegar and spear and reed;
   From that holy Body piercèd
      Blood and water forth proceed:
   Earth and stars and sky and ocean
      By that flood from stains are freed.

A - men.__

SOPRANOS & ALTOS

3. There-fore when th'ap-point-ed ful - ness Of__ the ho - ly time was come,__
6. Thou a - lone was count-ed wor - thy This__ world's Ran-som to sus - tain,__

Man.

He was sent who mak-eth all things Forth from God's e - ter - nal home:__
That a ship-wrecked race might ev - er Thus a port of re - fuge gain,__

vv. 4, 5, 7 & 8 on previous page

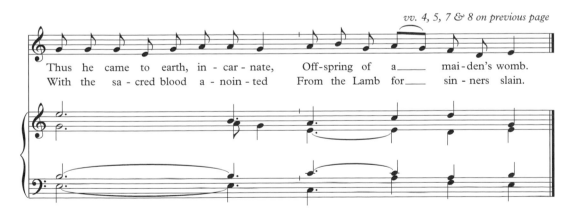

Thus he came to earth, in - car - nate, Off-spring of a__ mai-den's womb.
With the sa - cred blood a - noin - ted From the Lamb for__ sin - ners slain.

When I survey the wondrous cross

Isaac Watts (1674-1748)

Edward Miller (1731-1807)
Vv 3 & 5 arr. Tom Wiggall (b. 1978)

v.3 & 5 over page

SOPRANOS

3. See from_ his head, his hands, his feet, Sor-

-row and love flow min - gled down!_ Did

e'er such love and sor - row meet, Or

v.4 previous page

thorns com - pose so rich____ a crown?

72

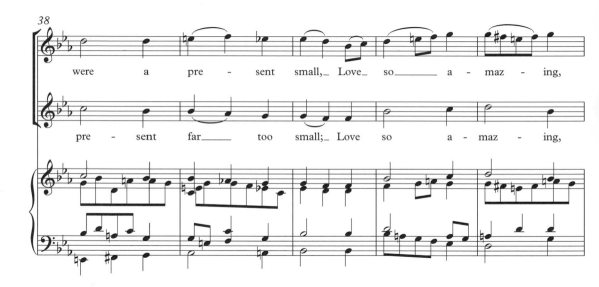

Hosanna to the son of David

Matthew 21: 9

Thomas Weelkes (c.1575-1623)
ed. Lionel Pike

74

Inggrediente Domino

Antiphon from
Palm Sunday Procession

George Malcolm (1917-98)

This piece may be sung as a processional, in which case repeat verses as many times as required.

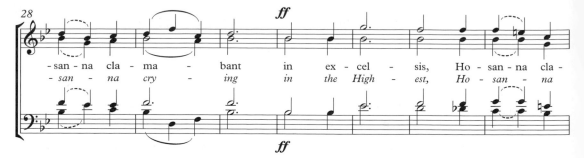

-san - na cla - ma - - bant in ex - cel - sis, Ho - san - na cla -
-san - na cry - ing in the High - est, Ho - san - na

ff

ff

Fine

-ma - bant in ex - cel - sis, in ex - cel - sis.
cry - ing in the High - est, in the High - est.

mf

2. Cum-que au - dis - set po - pu - lus quod Je - sus___ ve -
2. When all the peo - ple heard the___ cry that Je - sus___ was

mf

-ni - ret Hie - ro - so - ly - mam ex - i -
com - ing in - to___ Je - ru - sa - lem, they went

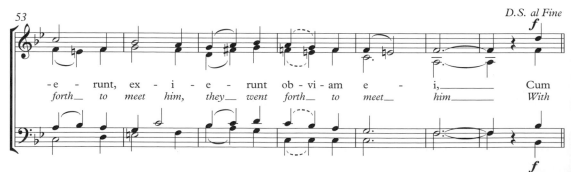

D.S. al Fine

f

-e - runt, ex - i - e - runt ob - vi - am e - i,___ Cum
forth___ to meet him, they___ went forth___ to meet___ him___ With

f

Palm Sunday Processional

Psalms 117 (118), 23 (24)

Plainsong melody
arr. David Hill (b.1957)

v.1 CANTOR

Con - fi - té - mi - ni Dó - mi - no quó - ni - am bo - nus,

repeat Antiphon 1

quó - ni - am in sáe - cu - lum mi - se - ri - cór - di - a e - ius.

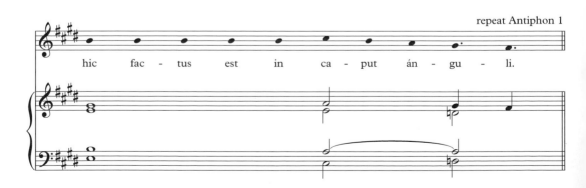

v.2 CANTOR

Lá - pi - dem quem re - pro - ba - vé - runt ae - di - fi - cán - tes,

repeat Antiphon 1

hic fac - tus est in ca - put án - gu - li.

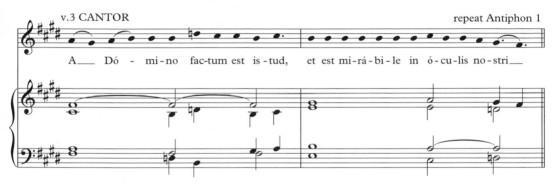

v.3 CANTOR — repeat Antiphon 1

A__ Dó - mi - no fac-tum est is -tud, et est mi-rá-bi - le in ó-cu-lis no-stri__

ANTIPHON 2

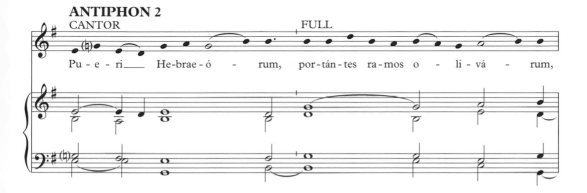

CANTOR — FULL

Pu - e - ri__ He-brae-ó - rum, por-tán-tes ra-mos o - li-vá - rum,

ob - vi - a - vé - runt__ Dó - mi - no, cla-mán - tes__ et

di - cén - tes: Ho-sán - na__ in ex-cél - sis.

84

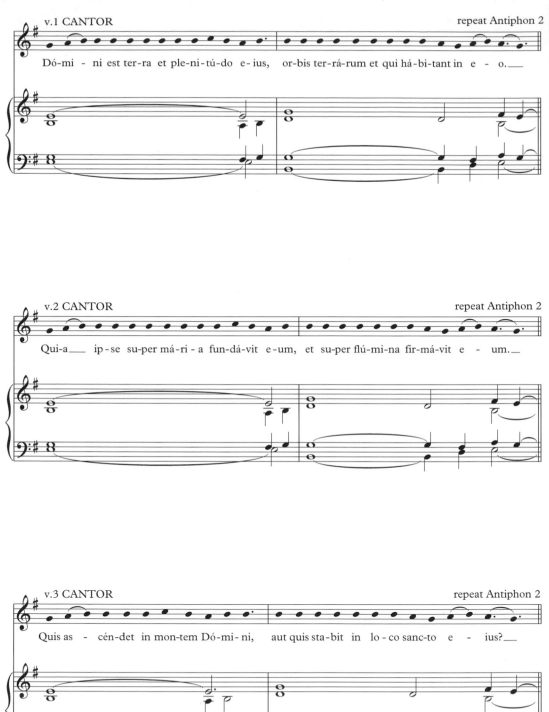

Dó-mi - ni est ter-ra et ple-ni-tú-do e - ius, or-bis ter-rá-rum et qui há-bi-tant in e - o.

Qui-a___ ip-se su-per má-ri - a fun-dá-vit e-um, et su-per flú-mi-na fir-má-vit e - um.___

Quis as - cén-det in mon-tem Dó-mi-ni, aut quis sta-bit in lo - co sanc-to e - ius?___

Ave verum

14th-century hymn

Svein Møller (1958-99)

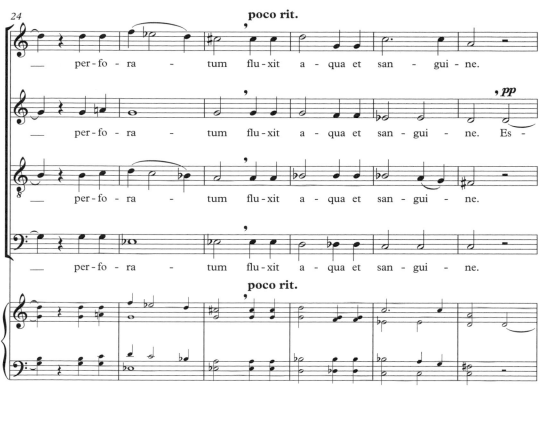

1996

Nos autem gloriari

Introit for Maundy Thursday

Grayston Ives (b. 1948)

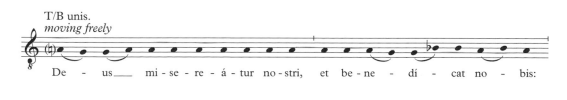

Translation

But as for us, it behoveth us to glory in the cross of our Lord Jesus Christ, in whom is our salvation, our life and resurrection, by whom we were saved and obtained our freedom.
God be merciful unto us and bless us: and show us the light of his countenance, and be merciful unto us.

In monte Oliveti

Matthew 26:39

Giovanni Croce (1557-1609)

* Source has C B♭ B♮ B♮ for first four notes of T.

O salutaris Hostia

Hymn for the feast of Corpus Christi
Thomas Aquinas (1227-74)

David Hill (b. 1957)

O sacrum convivium

Magnificat antiphon at Second Vespers,
Feast of Corpus Christi

Grayston Ives (b. 1948)

Available separately from Encore Publications, Juglans House, Brenchley Road, Matfield, Kent TN12 7DT, UK
www.encorepublications.com

da - tur._____

no - bis___ pi - gnus___ da - tur._____

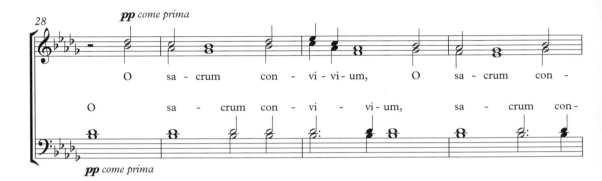

O sa - crum con - vi - vi - um, O sa - crum con -

O sa - crum con - vi - vi - um, sa - crum con -

- vi - vi - um___

in quo Chri-stus su - mi - tur, in quo Chri-stus

- vi - vi - um___

su - mi - tur, in___ quo___ Chri - stus___ su - mi - tur.

On the Mount of Olives

Matthew 26: 30, 39, 41

Ralph Allwood (b. 1950)

* Parts should be equally divided among voices.

Dedicated to
Their Royal Highnesses The Duke & Duchess of Cambridge
with respectful good wishes

Ubi caritas

Composed for the Marriage of His Royal Highness Prince William of Wales, K.G. with Miss Catherine Middleton
and first performed by the Choirs of Westminster Abbey and Her Majesty's Chapel Royal, St James's Palace,
conducted by James O'Donnell, at Westminster Abbey, Friday, 29th April 2011.

Where charity and love are, God is there.
Christ's love has gathered us into one.
Let us rejoice and be pleased in Him.
Let us fear, and let us love the living God.
And may we love each other with a sincere heart.

Hymn for Maundy Thursday   Paul Mealor (b. 1975)

104

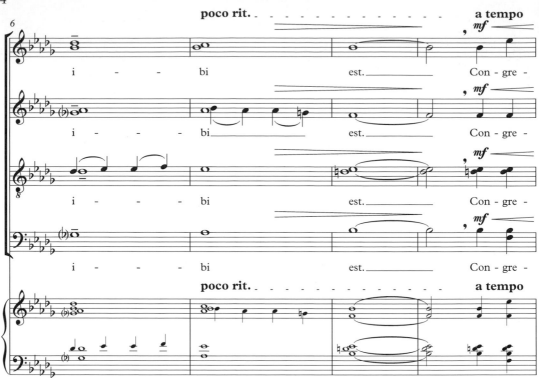

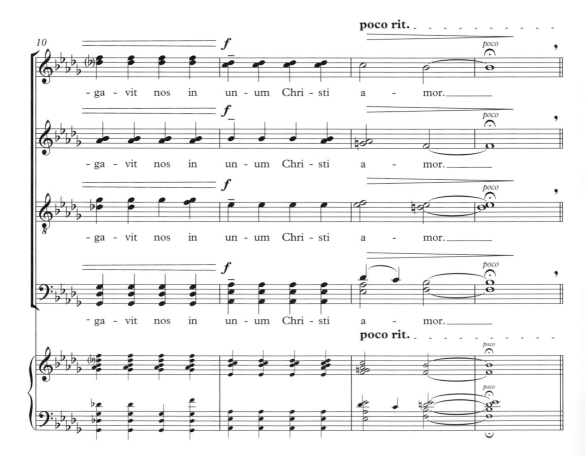

* Bracketed notes are optional divisi.

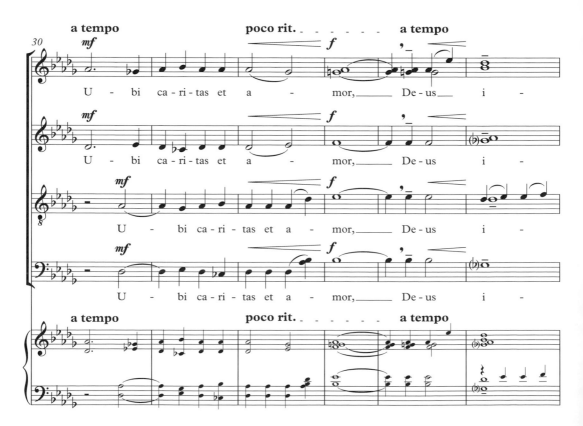

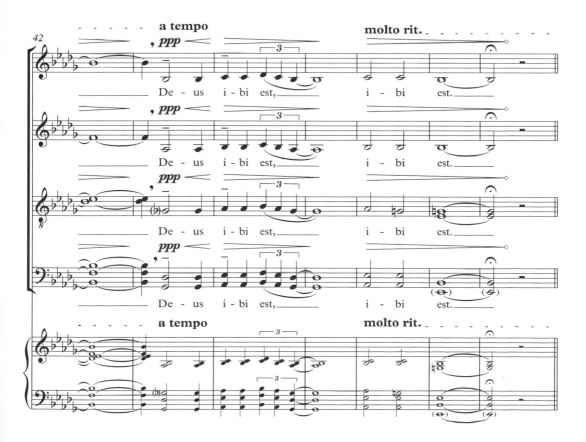

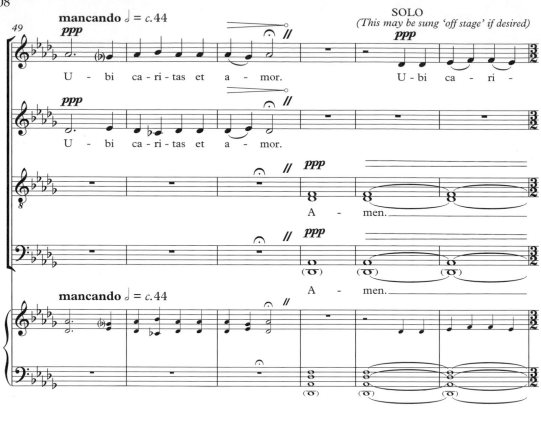

Crucifixus a 6

from the Nicene Creed

Antonio Lotti (c.1667-1740)

Gethsemane

William Tappan (1794-1849)

Adam Harvey (b. 1964)

-el wres-tles, lone, with fears; E'en the dis-ci-ple that he loved Heeds

-el___ wres-tles, lone, with fears; E'en the dis-ci-ple that he loved Heeds

-el wres-tles, lone, with fears; Dis - ci - ple that_ he loved Heeds

-el wres-tles, lone,_ with fears; Dis - ci - ple that he loved Heeds

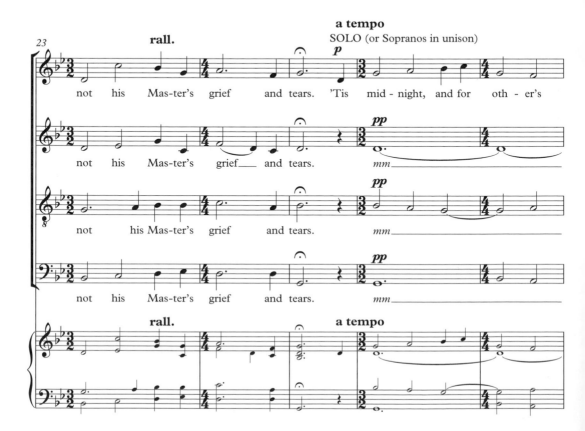

a tempo

rall. SOLO (or Sopranos in unison)
p

not his Mas-ter's grief and tears. 'Tis mid - night, and for oth - er's

pp
not his Mas-ter's grief___ and tears. mm___

pp
not his Mas-ter's grief and tears. mm___

pp
not his Mas-ter's grief and tears. mm___

rall. **a tempo**

guilt The Man of Sor-rows weeps in blood; Yet he, that hath in an - guish

knelt, Is not for - sak-en by his God. 'Tis mid - night, from the

In manus tuas

John 6: 30

Thomas Tallis (c.1505-1585)

for Benjamin Nicholas and the choir of the Abbey School, Tewkesbury

121

The Two Adams

John Donne (1572-1631)
from *Hymn to God, my God, in my Sickness*

Christopher Borrett (b.1985)

for Tilly
first performed by the Choir of All Saints Church, Fulham

My Lord is alone

Words & music:
Jonathan Wikeley (b. 1979)

* Smaller choirs may sing all verses to the harmony of the second and third verses.

power of his love comes stream-ing__ down, My Lord is crowned with a wreath of thorns.
power of his love comes stream-ing__ down, My Lord is pierced with a rust-y spear.

1.
O Lord, Come to me, Take my hand, Lead me home. 3. My

2. S. Solo
O Lord,__ Come__ to me, Take__ my hand,__ Lead me

O Lord, Come to me, Take my hand, Lead me home. 4. My

4. My

home.

Lord hangs high on a lone-ly__ cross, My Lord hangs__ high on a lone-ly cross, And

4. My Lord hangs high on a lone-ly cross, My Lord hangs high on a lone-ly

Lord hangs high on a lone-ly cross, My Lord hangs high on a lone-ly cross, And

39

all for the love of a sin-ner like__ me, The power of his love comes__

cross, And all for the love of a sin-ner like__ me, The power of his

all for the love of a sin-ner like me, The power of his love comes

42

stream - ing__ down, My Lord hangs high on a lone - ly cross.

love comes stream - ing__ down, My Lord hangs high on a lone - ly

stream - ing down, My Lord hangs high on a lone - ly cross.

45 **pp** *without expression*

S. O Lord, Come to me, Take my hand, Lead me home.

A. **pp** *without expression*
O Lord, Come to me, Take my hand, Lead me home.

pp *without expression*

T. cross. O Lord, Come to me,

pp *without expression*

B. O Lord, Come to me,

(for rehearsal only)

Stabat Mater

13th-century hymn

Juan Gutiérrez de Padilla
(c.1590-1664)

for the Men's Choir of the Community of Jesus, Orleans, Massachusetts

Steal away to Jesus

Spiritual

arr. Dale Adelmann (b. 1961)

This arrangement was originally labelled AATTBB

(1) The final 't' in 'ain't' and 'got' should be sung as a glottal stop.

* glissando
(2) To heighten the effect of the sforzando, close immediately to the 'n' of 'thunder',
but care must be taken not to rush into the final syllable.

(3) *Legatissimo*: slurred crotchets should be sung with slight
stresses on beats one and three, unstressed on beats two and four.

Holy Saturday 1990

The Reproaches

Liber Usualis

Colin Mawby (b. 1936)

The Reproaches

Liber Usualis

Tomás Luis de Victoria (1548–1611)

* If required, this piece may be sung full throughout.

144

repeat section B

Quid ul - tra dé - bu - i fá - ce - re_ ti - bi,_ et non_ fe - ci?_

E - go qui - dem plan - tá - vi_ te ví - ne - am me - am_ spe -

-ci - o - sís - si - mam: et_ tu_ fa - cta_ es mi - hi ni - mis a - má - ra:

a - ce - to_ nam - que si - tim me - am po - tá - sti:_

et_ lán - ce - a per - fo - rá - sti la - tus_ Sal - va - tá - ri tu - o._

repeat section **B**

E - go_ pro - pter te fla - gel - lá - vi Ae - gyp - tum cum pri - mo - gé - ni - tis su - is:

et tu_ me fla - gel - lá - tum_ tra - di - dí - sti._

repeat section **A**

E - go_ te e - du - xi de Ae - gyp - to, de - mér - so Pha - ra - ó - ne in Ma - re Ru - brum:

et tu_ me tra - di - dí - sti prin - cí - pi - bus_ sa - cer - dó - tum._

repeat section **A**

E - go_ an - te te a - pé - ru - i ma - - re:

et tu_ a - pe - ru - í - sti lán - ce - a_ la - tus me - um._

repeat section **A**

146

E - go___ an - te te prae - í - vi in co - lúm - na nu - bis:

et tu___ me du - xí - sti ad prae - tó - ri - um Pi - lá - ti.___

repeat section **A**

E - go___ te pa - vi man - na per de - sér - - tum:

et tu___ me ce - ci - dí - sti á - la - pis___ et fla - gél - lis.___

repeat section **A**

E - go___ te po - tá - vi a - qua sa - lú - tis de pe - tra:

et tu___ me po - tá - sti fel - le___ et a - cé - to.___

repeat section **A**

E - go___ prop - ter te Cha - na - nae - ó - rum re - ges per - cús - si:

et tu___ per - cus - sí - sti a - rún - di - ne___ ca - put me - um.___

repeat section **A**

E - go___ de - di ti - bi scep - trum re - gá - le:

et tu___ de - dí - sti cá - pi - ti me - o spí - ne - am co - ró - nam.___

repeat section **A**

E - go___ te ex - al - tá - vi ma - gna vir - tú - - te:

et tu___ me sus - pen - dí - sti in pa - tí - bu - lo Cru - cis.___

repeat section **A**

Were you there when they crucified my Lord?

Spiritual
arr. Stephen Jackson (b. 1951)

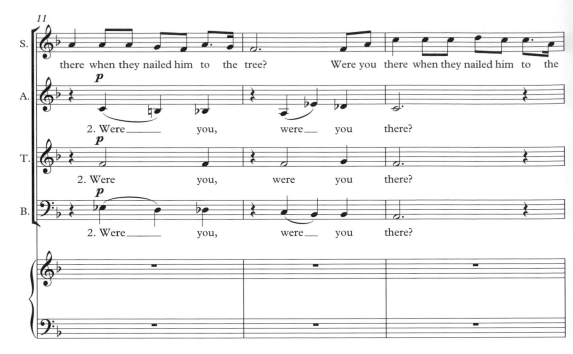

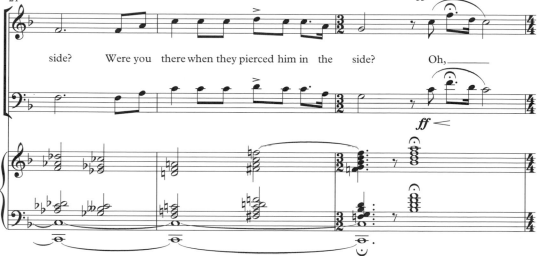

19 April 2011

Go down, Moses

Spiritual
arr. Richard Allain (b. 1965)

* May be performed down a tone.
** Solos optional

-pressed so hard they could not stand,_ Let my peo-ple go. Go down,

Mo-ses, 'way down in E-gypt's lan',____ Tell_ ole____ Pha-raoh__ to

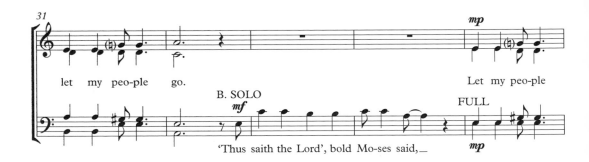

let my peo-ple go.

Let my peo-ple

B. SOLO

'Thus saith the Lord', bold Mo-ses said,_

go,

Let my peo-ple go.

B. SOLO

'If not, I'll smite your first-born dead'._

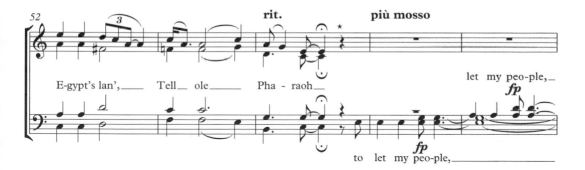

* If only SATB are available, this section to the end may be sung by S1, A1, T1 and B2.

Easter Troparion

from the Eastern Orthodox Rite

Loud and strong

SOPRANO
ALTO

TENOR
BASS

Christ is ris - en from the dead, tramp - ling down death by

death, and to those in the tomb be - stow - ing life.

x3

CANTOR: Christ is risen! (*f*, *shouted*)
FULL: He is risen indeed! (*f*, *shouted*)
CANTOR: Christ is risen! (*ff*)
FULL: He is risen indeed!
CANTOR: Christ is risen! (*fff*)
FULL: He is risen indeed!

Kris - stos vas-skrie - sye iz myert -vykh, smer - ti - yu smert pa -
Хрис - тос вос-кре - се изъ мерт - вихъ, смер - ті - ю смерт по -
Chris - tos a - nes - ti ek nek - rone, tha - na - toe tha - na - ton pa - ti -
Χρισ - τος α - νεσ - τι εκ νεκ - ρων, θα - να - τω θα - να - τον πα - τι -

x3

- prav,_____ i su - shchim va gra - biekh zhi - vot__ da - ra - vav.
- правъ,_____ И су - щымъ во гро - ъехъ__ жи - вотъ да - ро-вавъ.
- sas,_____ Kai tois en tois mnee-ma - si zoe-ee cha - ri - sa-men - os.
- σας,_____ Και τοις εν τοις μνη - μα - σι ζω - ην χα - ρι - σα - μεν - ος.

CANTOR: Khristos vasskriesye! (*f*, *shouted*)
FULL: Va Istinu vasskriesye! (*f*, *shouted*)
CANTOR: Khristos vasskriesye! (*ff*)
FULL: Va Istinu vasskriesye!
CANTOR: Khristos vasskriesye! (*fff*)
FULL: Va Istinu vasskriesye!

CANTOR: Christos anesti! (*f*, *shouted*)
FULL: Alithos anesti! (*f*, *shouted*)
CANTOR: Christos anesti! (*ff*)
FULL: Alithos anesti!
CANTOR: Christos anesti! (*fff*)
FULL: Alithos anesti!

* The English text should be sung three times, increasing in loudness each time, followed by the shouted responses. This should be followed by the texts in Russian and Greek.

Song for Athene

from the Funeral Service of
the Eastern Orthodox Church
& William Shakespeare (c. 1564-1611)

John Tavener (b. 1944)

Very tender, with great inner stillness and serenity

($\bullet$ = *c.* 56-60)

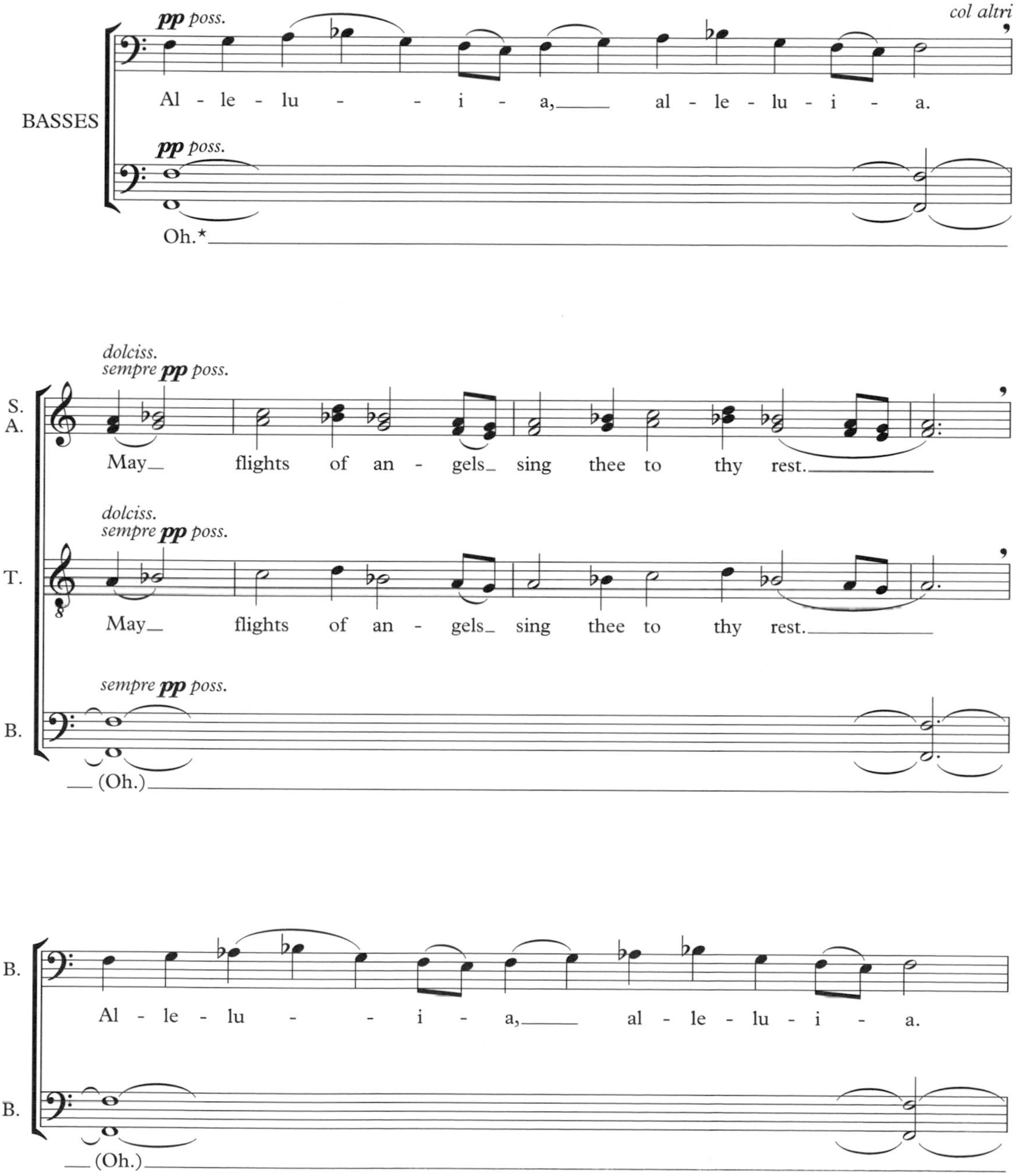

* 'Oh' as in the 'o' of 'log'. Breathe when necessary, but not simultaneously.

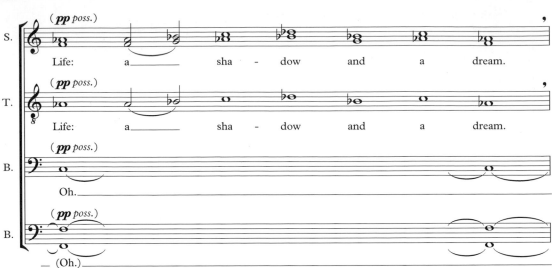

With resplendent joy in the Resurrection

S. *molto f*
Come, en - joy re - wards and_ crowns I have_ pre - pared_____ for_ you.

S.
A. *f*
Oh.

A. *molto f*
Come, en - joy re - wards and_ crowns I have_ pre - pared_____ for_ you.

T. *molto f*
Come, en - joy re - wards and_ crowns I have_ pre - pared_____ for_ you.

T. *f*
Oh.

B. *molto f*
Come, en - joy re - wards and_ crowns I have_ pre - pared_____ for_ you.

B. *f molto sonore*
Oh._____

rit.

B. *pp poss.*
Al - le - lu - i - a,___ al - le - lu - i - a,___ al - le - lu - i - a.

B. *pp poss.*
_ (Oh.)_____

Bermuda/Naldretts
11 April 1993

In loving memory of James Edward Colling Allen

A Thin Place
Anthem for the Easter Vigil

Words and music:
Jonathan Wikeley (b. 1979)

This piece may also be sung at Christmas, substituting the words 'Where Jesus Christ is born' in bars 32-34.

place:_____ Where God stretch-es out his hand, And we___ but

thin place, this is a thin place, this is a thin place,

need to take it._____

This, this is a thin place,

this is a thin place.

Where Christ our Lord is ris'n, And ev' - ry-thing, ev' - ry-thing,

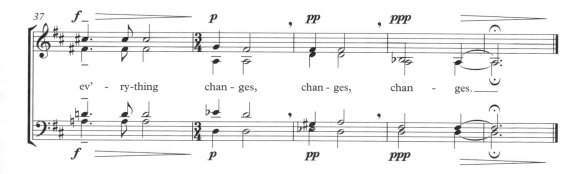

ev' - ry-thing chan - ges, chan - ges, chan - ges._____

Alleluia! Alleluia!

Christopher Wordsworth (1807-1885)

Arthur Sullivan (1842-1900)
Descant arrangements:
Richard Marlow (1939-2013)

1. Al - le - lu - ia! Al - le - lu - ia! Hearts to heav'n and voi - ces raise:

Sing to God a hymn of glad - ness, Sing to God a hymn of praise;

He who on the cross a vic - tim For the world's sal - va - tion bled,

Je - sus Christ, the King of glo - ry, Now is ris - en from the dead.

17

S.1: 2. Christ is ris - en, Christ the__ first - fruits of the har - vest_ field, Which_

S.2 / A.: 2. Christ is ris - en, Christ the first-fruits Of the ho - ly har - vest field,

21

__ will all__ its__ full a - bun-dance At his se - cond_ com-ing yield; Then_ the

Which will all its full a - bun-dance At his se - cond com - ing yield;

25

gold - en ears_ of__ boun-teous har - vest Will their_ heads be - fore him wave Ri - pened

Then the gold - en ears of har - vest Will their heads be - fore him wave,

29

by his glo - rious_ sun-shine From_ the__ deep-est fur - rows of the grave.

Ri - pened by his glo - rious sun - shine From the fur - rows of the grave.

166

At the Lamb's high feast we sing

From a Latin Breviary hymn
Trans. Richard Campbell (1814-1868)

Melody: from J. Hinzte (1622-1702)
Harmonisation: J. S. Bach (1685-1750)
Descant arrangements:
Richard Marlow (1939-2013)

1. At the Lamb's high feast we sing Praise to our vic - to - rious King:
Who hath washed us in the tide Flow - ing from his pier - cèd side;
Praise we him whose love di - vine Gives the guests his blood for wine,
Gives his bo - dy for the feast, Love the Vic - tim, Love the Priest.

170

53

_____ sin's_ death do thou _____ set free, Souls_ re - born dear Lord, in thee. Hymns_ of

_____ sin's_ death do_ thou_ set free, Souls_____ re - born, dear Lord, in thee. Hymns_

From sin's death do thou set free, Souls re - born, dear Lord, in thee. Hymns_

57

glo - ry, songs_ of__ thanks and praise, Fa - ther, un - to thee_ we_ joy - ful raise. Ris-

_____ of_ glo - ry,_____ songs_ of praise, Fa - ther, un - to thee we raise. Ris-

Hymns of glo - ry, songs of praise, Fa - ther, un - to thee we raise.

61

- en_ Lord, all praise to thee, With_ the Ho - ly Spi - rit ev - er be.

- en Lord,_____ all_ praise_ to_ thee, With__ the Spi - rit_ ev - er_ be.

Ris - en Lord, all praise to thee, Ev - er with the Spi - rit be.

Christ being raised from the dead

Romans 6:9
Psalm 98: 1

Philip Moore (b. 1943)

Canterbury, 26 October 1972

Christ now is risen

Easter hymn

Melchior Vulpius (c.1570-1615)

Christ the Lord is risen

Isaac Watts (1674-1748)

Old German melody
Gesang- unt Gebetbuch für die Diöcese Trier (1871)
arr. Matthew O'Donovan (b. 1981)

-mor - tal Lamb, Thine ar - mies trod_ the temp - ter down; 'Twas by thy word and

power - ful name they gained the bat - tle and_ re-nown. Al - le - lu-ia, al - le - lu - ia!

3. Christ the Lord_ is ri - sen! Re-joice, ye heavens! let

ev-'ry star shine with new glo - ries round the sky! Saints, while ye sing the

heav'n-ly war, raise your Re-deem-er's name_ on high! Al - le - lu - ia, al-

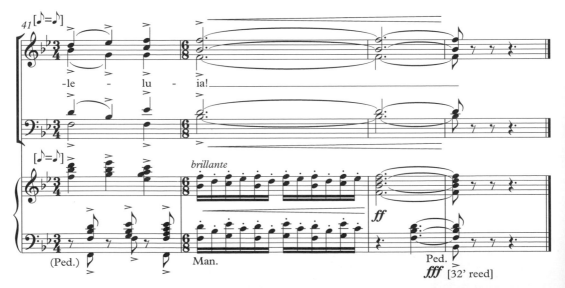

-le - lu - ia!

Easter Carol

17th-century Easter carol

Jamie W. Hall (b. 1983)

Dum transisset Sabbatum

Third responsory at
Matins on Easter Sunday

John Taverner (c.1498-1545)

This edition transposed up a tone.

186

* *Source has two crotchets here.*

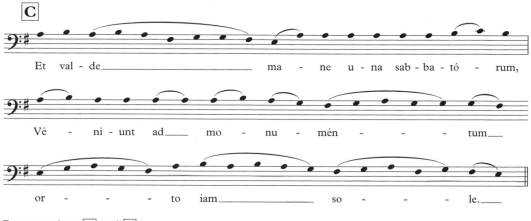

C

Et val - de_____ ma - ne u - na sab - ba - tó - rum,

Vé - ni - unt ad___ mo - nu - mén - - - tum___

or - - - to iam_____ so - - - le.___

Repeat sections A and B

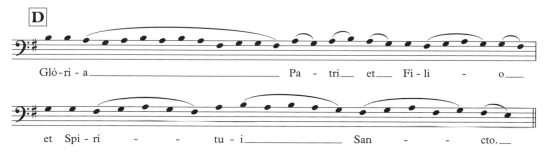

D

Gló - ri - a_____ Pa - tri et___ Fí - li - o___

et Spi - rí - - tu - i_____ San - - cto.___

Repeat section B

for Timothy Brown and Robinson College Chapel Choir

I got me flowers

an Easter anthem

George Herbert (1593-1633)

Jeremy Thurlow (b. 1967)

Jesus Christ is risen today

Lyra Davidica 1708

Adapted from a melody
in Lyra Davidica 1708
arr. Matthew O'Donovan (b. 1981)

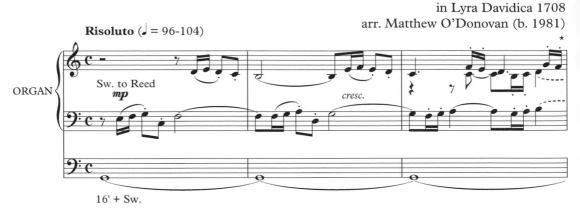

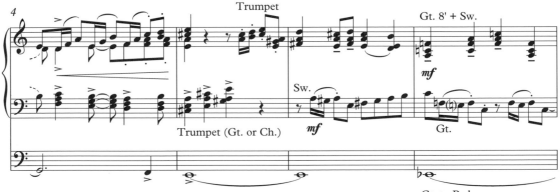

* Optional cut to bar 14. Alternatively the introduction to every verse may be omitted.

A version of this piece for organ and brass quintet is available on request from the publishers.

VOICES & ORGAN

1. Je - sus Christ is ris'n to - day,___ Al - - le - lu - ia!

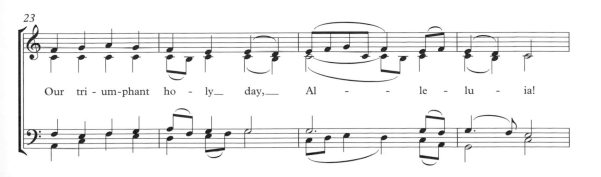

Our tri - um - phant ho - ly___ day,___ Al - - le - lu - ia!

Who did once, up - on the cross, Al - - le - lu - ia!

Suf - fer to re - deem our loss.__ Al - - le - lu - ia!

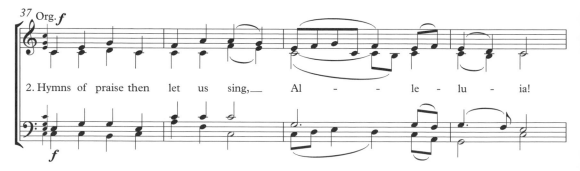

2. Hymns of praise then let us sing,__ Al - - le - lu - ia!

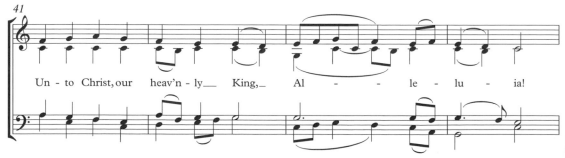

Un - to Christ, our heav'n - ly__ King,__ Al - - le - lu - ia!

Who en - dured the_ cross and grave, Al - - le - lu - ia!

Sin - ners_ to re - deem and save._ Al - - le - lu - ia!

Gt. *mf*

(Gt. foundations
with Sw. coupled)

FULL
mf

3. But the pains that he en - dured_ Al - - le - lu - ia!

add

Our sal - va - tion hath pro - cured;___ Al - - le - lu - ia!

DESCANT

A - bove,___ he's King, Al - - le - lu - ia!

ALL OTHER VOICES

Now a - bove the sky he's King, Al - - le - lu - ia!

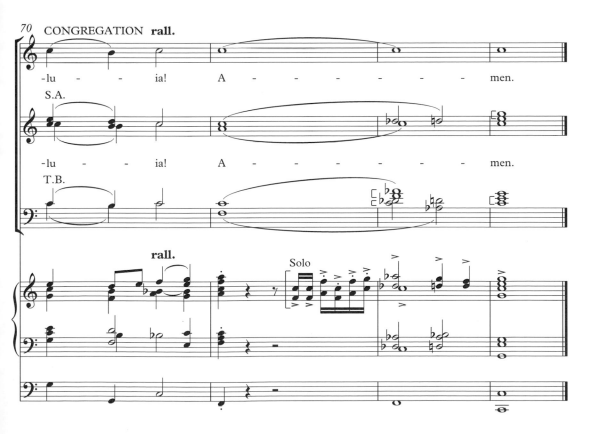

this arrangement in affectionate memory of Philip Jones

Lord of the Dance

Sydney Carter (1915-2004)

Adapted from a Shaker melody
by Sydney Carter (1915-2004)
arr. Stephen Jackson (b. 1951)

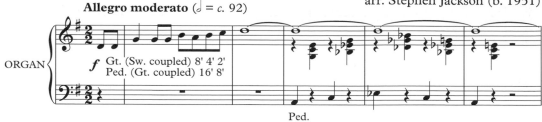

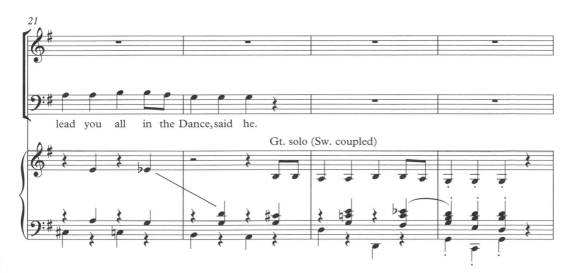

danced for the scribe and the pha-ri-see, But they would not dance, and they would-n't fol-low me, I

danced for the fish-er-men, for James and John, They came with me and the Dance went on.

Dance, then, wher-ev-er you may be, I am the Lord of the Dance, said he, And I'll

lead you all wher-ev-er you may be, And I'll lead you all in the Dance, said he.

danced on the Sab-bath and I cured the lame, The ho-ly peo-ple___ said it was a shame, They

back. They bu - ried my bo - dy and they thought I'd gone, But

Man.

I am the Dance and I still go on.

Gt.

Ped.

+ Gt. to Ped.

reduce

add full Sw. (box closed)

for Geoffrey Webber and the choir of Pusey House

May Carol

Trad. Easter carol
arr. Peter John Still (b. 1958)

* In both full sections the altos and tenors should match tone as far as possible.

bless you__ all, both great__ and small, And I

So God bless you__ all, both great__ and small,_____ And I

So God bless you__ all, both great__ and small, And I

gone; So_____ God_ bless you great and small, And I

wish you a joy-ful May._____

wish you a joy-ful, joy - ful,_____ a joy-ful May.

wish__ you a joy-ful, joy - - - ful May.

wish you a joy-ful, joy - - ful May.

April 1983

To Ursula and Martin Watson

My beloved spake

Song of Solomon 2: 10-13

Patrick Hadley (1899–1973)

216

* Bars 10-21 should ideally be unaccompanied, but should it be found advisable, some discreet assistance may be rendered by reference to the small notes. The large notes in this section refer to passages which occur in the full orchestral score.

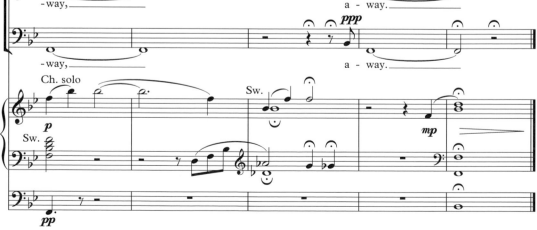

Now the green blade riseth

J. M. C. Crum (1872-1958)

Trad. French carol
arr. David Terry (b. 1975)

wheat that_ spring-eth green.

In the grave they laid_ him,

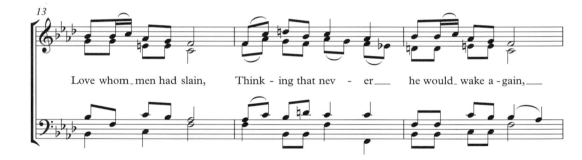

Love whom_ men had slain, Think - ing that nev - er___ he would_ wake a - gain,___

Laid in the earth like grain that sleeps un- seen: Love is come a - gain_ like_

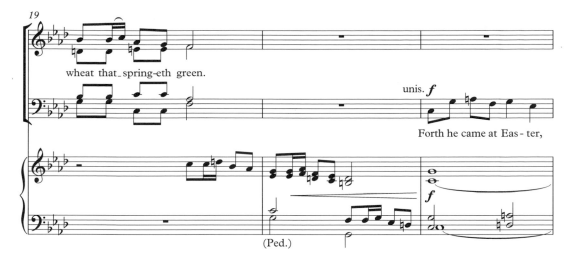

wheat that spring-eth green.

unis. *f*
Forth he came at Eas - ter,

(Ped.)

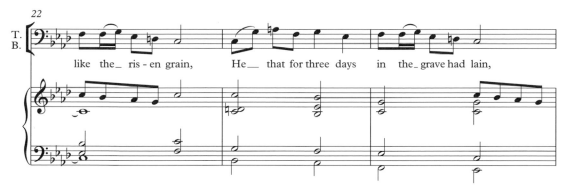

T.
B.

like the ris - en grain, He that for three days in the grave had lain,

Quick from the dead, my ris - en Lord is seen: Love is come a - gain like

rit.

wheat that spring-eth green.

p

Man.

a tempo

SOPRANO

When our hearts are win - try, griev-ing— or in pain, Thy— touch can call us

a tempo Solo flute

back to— life a-gain.

Fields of our hearts, that dead and bare have been:

SOPRANO & ALTO

rit.

Love is come a-gain like wheat that— spring-eth green.

Solo

Ped.

O for a lay!

George Ratcliffe Woodward
(1848-1934)

Melody: Bohemian Brethren, 1566
harm. Charles Wood (1866-1926)

Sing ye to the Lord

Exodus 15: 21, 4 and
Robert Campbell (1814-68)

Edward Bairstow (1874-1946)

Pha-raoh's char - iots and his host_____ hath he

Gt. or Full Sw. *f*

Ped.

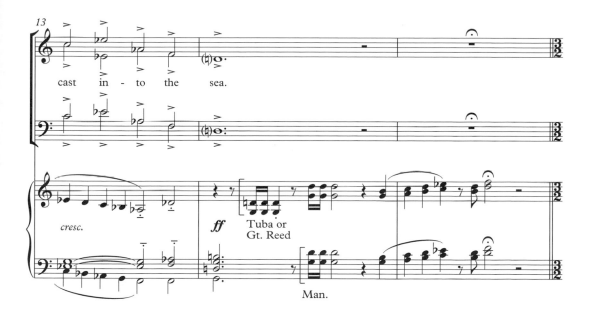

cast in - to the sea.

cresc.

ff   Tuba or
        Gt. Reed

Man.

Con moto moderato ♩ = 72

unis. *mf*

T.
B.

Might - y vic - tim from the sky,___ Hell's fierce pow'rs___ be-neath thee

Con moto moderato ♩ = 72

mf Gt. Diaps.

Ped.

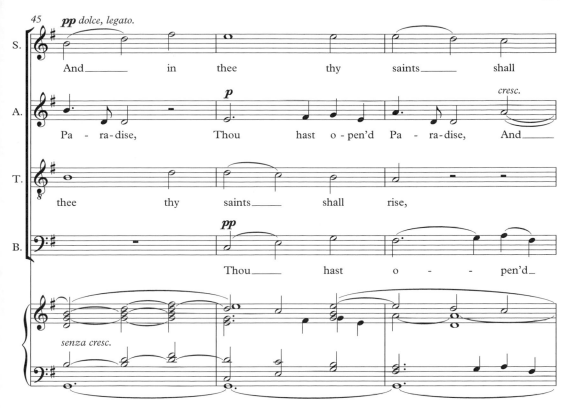

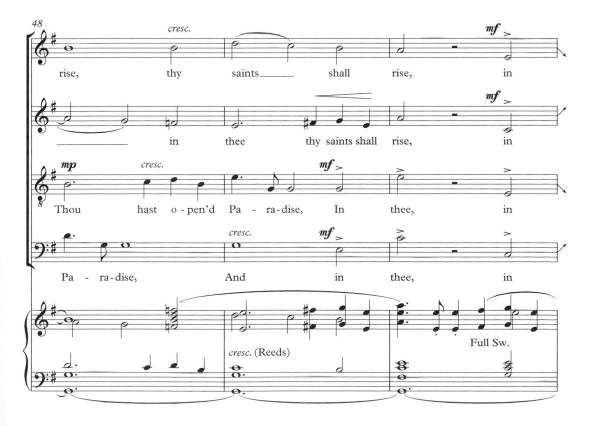

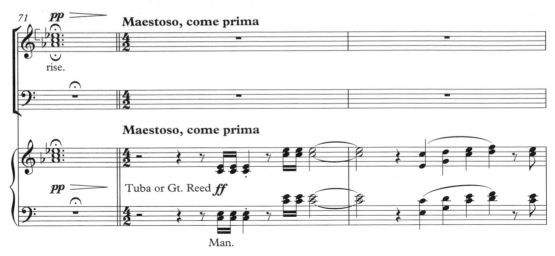

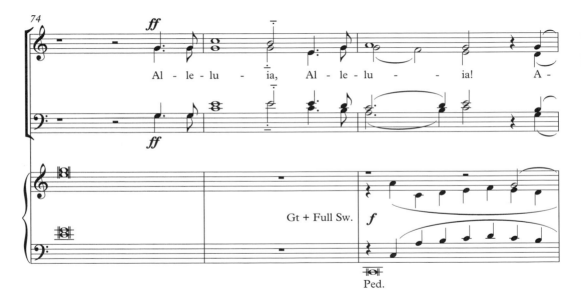

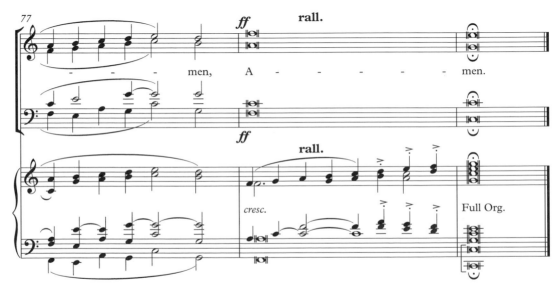

à Monsieur le Chanoine R. MOISSENET,
Maître de Chapelle de la Cathédrale de Dijon

Surrexit a mortuis

Easter respond

Charles-Marie Widor (1844-1937)
Organ part realised by
Richard Hills (b. 1980)

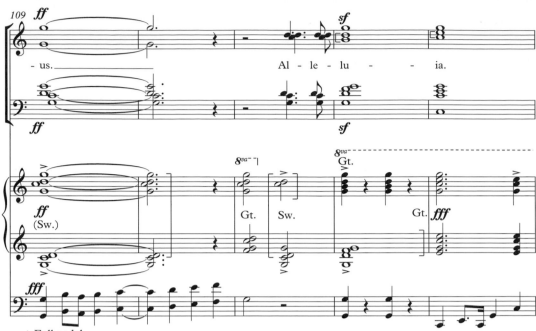

+ Full pedal

Surrexit pastor bonus

Easter respond

Orlando di Lasso (1532-94)

Thine be the glory

Edmond Budry (1854–1932)
Trans. Richard Hoyle (1875–1939)

Georg Frideric Handel (1685–1759)
arr. Peter Miller (b. 1946)

ORGAN

Tuba 8'

Sw.

Man.

Ped.

VOICES & ORGAN

S.
A.

T.
B.

1. Thine be the glo - ry, ris - en, con-quering Son,
2. Lo, Je - sus meets us, ris - en from the tomb;

End - less is the vic - t'ry thou o'er death hast won;
Lov - ing - ly he greets us, scat - ters fear and gloom;

An - gels in bright rai - ment rolled the stone a - way,
Let the Church with glad - ness hymns of tri - umph sing,

Kept_ the_ fold - ed grave - clothes where thy_ bo - dy lay.
For_ her_ Lord now liv - eth, death hath_ lost its sting.

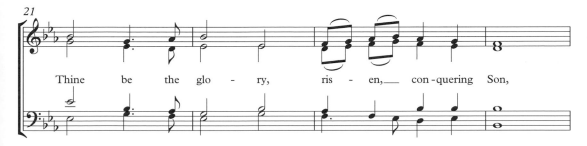

Thine be the glo - ry, ris - en,_ con - quering Son,

End - less_ is the vic - t'ry thou o'er_ death hast won.

small notes organ only

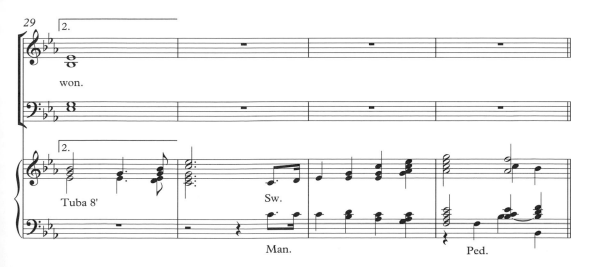

won.

Tuba 8'   Sw.

Man.   Ped.

FULL UNISON

3. No more we doubt thee, glor - ious__ Prince of Life;

Life__ is__ nought with - out thee: aid us__ in our strife,

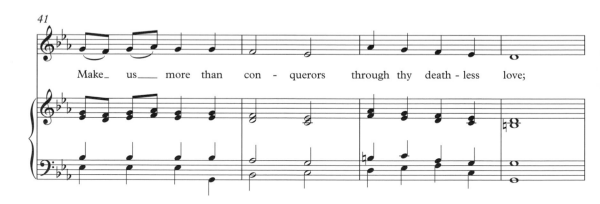

Make__ us__ more than con - querors through thy death - less love;

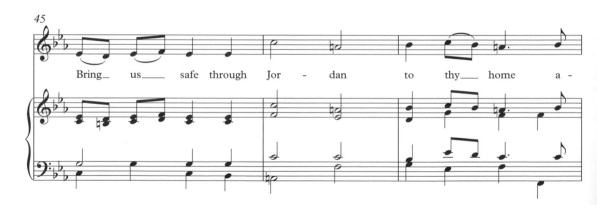

Bring__ us__ safe through Jor - dan to thy__ home a -

'Tis the day of Resurrection

St. John Damascene (c.750)
Trans. J.M. Neale (1818-1866)

Old French Noël
harm. Edmund Sedding (1835-1868)

Light and flowing

SOPRANO
ALTO

'Tis the day of Re-sur-rec-tion: Earth, tell it out a-broad!
The Pass-ov-er of glad-ness, The Pass-ov-er of God!

TENOR
BASS

From death to life e-ter-nal, From earth un-to the sky, Our

Christ hath brought us ov-er With hymns of vic-to-ry.

2. Our hearts be pure from evil,
That we may see aright
The Lord in rays eternal
Of Resurrection-light:
And, list'ning to his accents,
May hear, so calm and plain,
His own *All hail!* and hearing,
May raise the victor-strain.

3. Now let the heav'ns be joyful!
Let earth her song begin!
Let the round world keep triumph,
And all that is therein:
Let all things seen and unseen
Their notes of gladness blend,
For Christ the Lord hath risen,
Our Joy that hath no end.

for Leicester Cathedral Choir, Simon Headley and the Graff Orchestra of England

Ye choirs of new Jerusalem

St Fulbert of Chartres (c. 952-1028)
Trans. Robert Campbell (1814-68)

H.J. Gauntlett (1805-1876)
Vv 1, 2 & 6 arr. Christopher Johns (b. 1975)

258

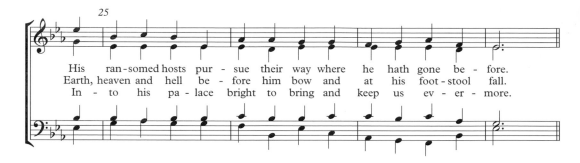